Inhalants=

John Bankston

 Enslow Publishers, Inc.
40 Industrial Road
Box 398
Berkeley Heights, NJ 07922
USA

http://www.enslow.com

Library of Congress Cataloging-in-Publication Data

Bankston, John, 1974–
    Inhalants=Busted! / John Bankston.
      p. cm. — (Busted!)
    Includes bibliographical references and index.
    ISBN 0-7660-2472-5
    1. Substance abuse—Juvenile literature. 2. Aerosol sniffing—Juvenile literature.
    3. Solvent abuse—Juvenile literature. 4. Youth—Substance use—Juvenile literature.
    I. Title. II. Series.
    HV4998B36 2006
    613.8—dc22

                                            2005029372

Printed in the United States of America

10 9 8 7 6 5 4 3 2 1

To Our Readers: We have done our best to make sure all Internet Addresses in this book were active and appropriate when we went to press. However, the author and the publisher have no control over and assume no liability for the material available on those Internet sites or on other Web sites they may link to. Any comments or suggestions can be sent by e-mail to comments@enslow.com or to the address on the back cover.

Every effort has been made to locate all copyright holders of material used in this book. If any errors or omissions have occurred, corrections will be made in future editions of this book.

Illustration Credits: Associated Press, pp. 44, 57; BananaStock, pp. 46–47, 61, 66–67, 76; Brand X Pictures, p. 37; Corbis, p. 71; Corel Corporation, pp. 30–31, 34; Courtesy of the DEA, p. 12; © 2005 JupiterImages, pp. 4–5, 8, 14–15, 25, 40 (top and bottom), 78–79; Courtesy of National Inhalant Prevention Coalition, pp. 18, 20; Steve Degenhardt, p. 42; stockbyte, p. 54.

Cover Illustration: Associated Press.

CONTENTS

CHAPTER ONE

DEADLY GAMES

Andrew Sandy was thirteen years old and he was an addict. He had been arrested for threatening his teacher, then he violated his probation by getting caught with marijuana and alcohol. Yet, his drug of choice was not purchased on a street corner or stolen from a liquor cabinet.

INHALANTS = BUSTED!

It came from an air conditioner.

Sandy was a "huffer." He got his high from inhaling chemicals, using Freon, a chemical compound containing carbon and fluorine, ripped from his parent's air-conditioning unit. He was seven years old when a friend showed him how. He had been hooked ever since.

For years, his mother did not know. Then one winter day in 2002, he finally confessed. "The abuse destroyed my son's life," she later admitted, but no matter how hard she tried, she could not get him to stop.[1]

Sandy lived in Calvert County, Maryland, a rural oasis between the hustle and bustle of Annapolis and the nation's capital. Homes are often separated by acres of forest bisected by

MYTH		FACT
Since these chemicals are everywhere, they must be safe.	VS.	Most chemicals require that they be used in ventilated areas. Inhaling them can cause permanent heart, lung, and brain damage or even death.

winding back roads. Yet Calvert County is growing. Jobs in Annapolis and Washington, D.C., have drawn thousands of new residents hoping to work in the city and live in the country. Their choice has a price.

John Mitchell is the director of Calvert County Substance Abuse Services. He says the county's growth has "exploded," and with it the rise of "two-parent, working families, where a lot of kids go home to an empty household. The commute from here to D.C. is at least an hour each way."[2]

Unsupervised, a few young adults made some bad decisions. The year before Sandy's confession to his mother, a Maryland adolescent survey reported some 11 percent of Calvert County eighth graders had experimented with inhalants.[3]

On the afternoon of March 13, 2002, Sandy took a garbage bag into his bedroom. Placing it over his head, he released Freon from the family air conditioner into the space, tightening the bag to keep the chemical from escaping.

This is extraordinarily risky. The Freon could not get out and oxygen could not get in. Every time Sandy got high, he risked suffocating. Sandy ignored the dangers. Deprived of oxygen, the

Many inhalant abusers wind up in the hospital or dead.

body begins to shut down. Eventually the heart and lungs stop working, and the brain dies.

Sandy had always managed to get the bag off in time. This time he was not so lucky.

By the time paramedics arrived, Sandy was unconscious. They worked feverishly to save his life as they raced to Calvert County Memorial Hospital, but it was too late. He died from lack of oxygen to the brain.

Every time a patient like Sandy arrives at an emergency room because of inhalant overdose, it is reported. In 2002, the year Sandy died, inhalant overdoses were 186 percent higher than in 2001. Although the slightly over one hundred reported deaths from inhalant overdoses every year is small compared to deaths from drugs like alcohol and heroin, experts believe the actual number is far higher. Some inhalant overdoses are not correctly identified, while many inhalant abusers go unrecognized.[4]

Sandy's death reflects a shocking increase in the abuse of inhalants by kids in their early teens and preteens. In the last two years alone, inhalant abuse among eighth graders like Sandy has risen by 18 percent. Even more frightening, inhalant

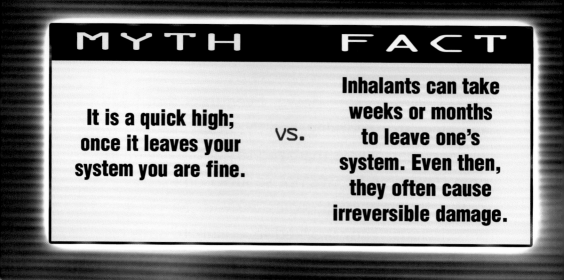

MYTH		FACT
It is a quick high; once it leaves your system you are fine.	VS.	Inhalants can take weeks or months to leave one's system. Even then, they often cause irreversible damage.

abuse among sixth graders during the same period has increased by 48 percent.[5]

As one law enforcement official points out, many such drug abusers have chosen a one-way street.

"[Huffers] usually don't get caught unless they die," Detective Jane Milne of the Family Services division of Montgomery County explains.[6]

Although abusers of inhalants experiment with different ways to get high, the chemicals they use are universally dangerous. They have warning labels graphically describing their risks. They are not supposed to be swallowed or left on the skin. If they get into your eyes, you are supposed to flush them with water for at least fifteen minutes. If a small amount is accidentally swallowed, the labels advise one to "immediately seek medical attention." Everything from gasoline to model airplane glue has specific precautions against inhaling; users are always told to keep the product in a well-ventilated area.

Since 1975, the Food and Drug Administration has required that consumer products like hair spray and cleaning fluids bear the label "Use only as directed; intentional misuse by deliberately concentrating and inhaling the contents can be harmful or fatal."[7]

Every year, the National Institute on Drug Abuse (NIDA) conducts a survey. They ask teens what drugs they have tried in the past year, and in the past month. They survey fifty thousand students in four hundred schools across the country.

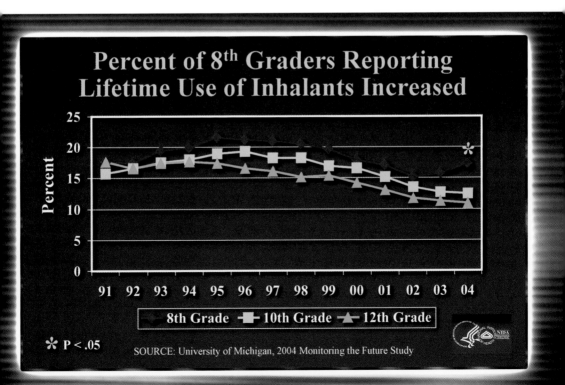

Percent of 8th Graders Reporting Lifetime Use of Inhalants Increased

8th Grade — 10th Grade — 12th Grade

* P < .05

SOURCE: University of Michigan, 2004 Monitoring the Future Study

INHALANTS = BUSTED!

According to the Monitoring the Future (MTF) survey, NIDA's nationwide annual survey of drug use among the nation's eighth, tenth, and twelfth graders, lifetime inhalant use by eighth graders increased significantly in 2004 after a long and substantial decline through 2002 in all three grades. Between 1995 and 2002, eighth graders' annual prevalence fell from 12.8 percent to 7.7 percent, "as an increasing proportion of students came to see inhalant use as dangerous," the survey reports.[8]

After 2002, that began to change. Annual prevalence rose significantly for eighth graders, from 7.7 percent to 8.7 percent from 2002

While inhalants have been around for many years, prescription medication like OxyContin, shown here, has just recently been made available. Inhalants and OxyContin are dangerous when abused.

to 2003. In 2004, eighth-graders' annual use was 9.6 percent.[9]

In late 2004, NIDA director Nora D. Volkow noted that the rise in inhalant abuse was "the only increase of any substance reported by MTF between 2002 and 2003."[10]

Over the last decade, as better information about the deadly dangers of drugs like cocaine, marijuana, alcohol, and ecstasy has reached young adults, their use has dramatically declined. Prescription drug abuse has also recently increased, but abused drugs like OxyContin and Vicodin were developed over the last decade. Inhalants have been around in one form or another for centuries.

Inhalants are easy to use and to find. Often they are already available in the user's home. Because of this, some young adults believe inhaling chemicals is just harmless fun.

This belief is wrong—dead wrong.

CHAPTER TWO

TOXIC CHEM LAB

It is not easy for a ten-year-old to get drugs.

Sure, illegal drugs may be available for sale everywhere. Dealers selling by elementary schools are busted nearly every day. But drugs cost money, and few fifth graders have the cash to support a habit.

INHALANTS = BUSTED!

Amy did not want her last name used when she spoke about her experience. Still, she wanted other kids to know what she went through, hoping they would not make the same mistake she did. Like lots of kids, she wanted to be accepted by the older crowd. Unfortunately, she thought huffing was the answer.

She had come across a group of girls inhaling gasoline. "We're huffing," one girl explained. "Would you like to try it?"

"I was scared and curious at the same time. I really wanted them to like me . . . so I said yes."

Her first time was terrifying: "The gas burned my throat and I started to feel dizzy and light headed. I was scared. I didn't know what was going on. Then I started hallucinating."[1]

Despite the negative experience, Amy was hooked. It took three years of family battles and several near fatal overdoses before she got treatment.

All drugs are tough to kick, but inhalants can be the worst. After all, they are everywhere. Even worse, many of the kids abusing inhalants are younger than other drug users.

Researchers in Australia noted that, "Unlike most other drugs, spray paints [and other inhalants] are cheap and accessible even to under eighteen year olds. Younger users also talked about the pleasures of being able to access their own drugs without needing the money or contacts to deal with the illicit drug market or to access alcohol."[2]

Inhalant abusers quickly find there is no such thing as a cheap high.

Looking back on teenage drug use, adults will often use the phrase "harmless experimentation." But there is nothing harmless about inhalants.

The drugs work quickly. Inhaled chemicals pass from the mouth or nose into the airways to the lungs. Only a few moments after the first inhalation, the chemicals travel through the bloodstream. They quickly come into contact with the cerebellum and cerebral cortex in the brain along with the central nervous system. The cerebellum controls movement, the cerebral cortex higher thought processes.

Inhalants are fat soluble, capable of being stored in the fat tissues of the user's body. The chemicals are attracted to myelin, an essential fatty tissue insulating the axons of the brain.

To understand the importance of myelin, picture the electrical cord that leads to appliances like

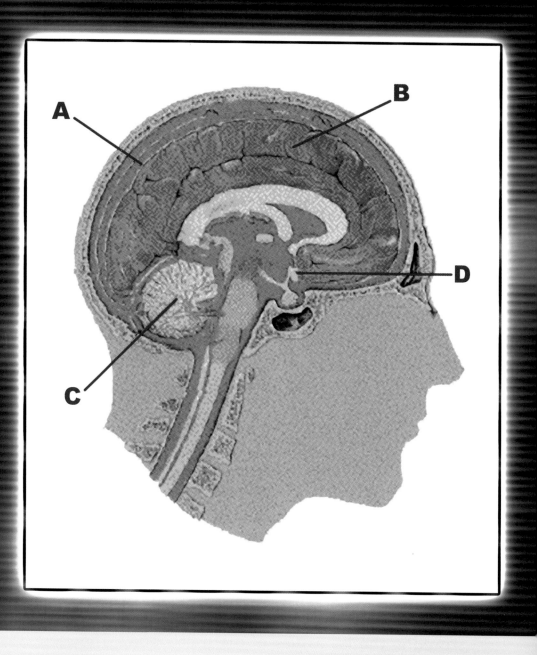

A BRAIN. The chemicals that are inhaled by abusers affect different parts of the brain. Many inhalants may dissolve the myelin sheath that surrounds brain cells, resulting in cell death.

B CEREBRAL CORTEX. Cell death here can result in permanent personality changes, memory problems, hallucinations, and learning disabilities.

C CEREBELLUM. This part of the brain controls balance and coordination. Loss of coordination and slurred speech can occur from inhalant abuse.

D OPHTHALMIC NERVE. Inhaling toluene may cause sight disorders.

lamps and microwaves. Plugged into an outlet, these cords carry the electricity that powers the appliance.

In your brain, axons are like electrical wires sending currents back and forth from your brain, messages that almost instantly control your legs when you walk, your mouth when you speak, and thousands of other tasks we do every day. Insulation surrounds the wires of an electrical cord, protecting you from an electric shock. Like insulation, myelin surrounds the brain's axons, but it also helps insure the rapid delivery and accuracy of the brain's signals.[3]

Inhalant abuse can permanently damage the myelin. Axons send messages throughout the brain. Damaged myelin can impair the transmission of those signals. An inhalant user may have problems walking or even talking. This damage could affect the user's eyesight and his or her hearing and mobility. Long-term users frequently have problems with their arms and legs. Often their limbs twitch uncontrollably; some have a hard time walking beyond a short distance.

As one researcher explained, brain damage "is the most recognized and reported chronic side effect of inhaled solvent abuse. Magnetic

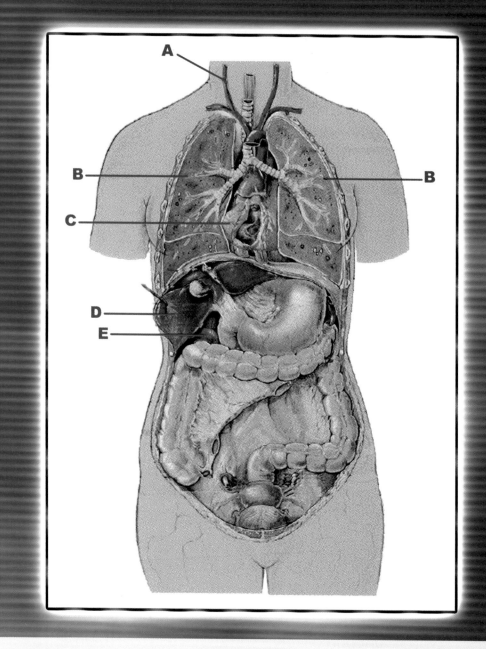

A BLOOD. Some chemicals such as nitrites and paint thinners block the oxygen-carrying capacity of the blood.

B LUNGS. Inhaling spray paint repeatedly can cause lung damage.

C HEART. Inhalant abuse can result in "sudden sniffing death syndrome." A sudden and unexpected disturbance of the heart's rhythm is the cause. All inhalants can produce sudden sniffing death syndrome.

D LIVER. Components of spray paints and correction fluid have been known to cause liver damage.

E KIDNEY. Toluene can impair the kidney's ability to control the amount of acid in the blood.

resonance imaging suggests that these white matter changes in chronic abusers are irreversible."[4]

Although they had died from numerous causes, the bodies of former chemical inhalers had one thing in common. During autopsies, pathologists had made a surprising discovery. Not only was the myelin in the brain damaged, so too were portions of the peripheral nervous system.[5]

This damage to nerve fibers resembled that of multiple sclerosis (MS) sufferers. An inflammatory disease of the central nervous system, MS sufferers endure similar damage to their myelin. This debilitating and frequently fatal disease is marked by a hardening of the soft tissues of both the brain and nerve fibers. There is currently no cure for MS.[6]

Brain scans of toluene abusers reveal dark spots, representing shrinkage of the tissue. This damage is clearly visible while the healthy brains of non inhalant abusers possess abundant brain tissue in the same area.

Besides damaging the brain and nervous system, toluene also affects the heart, lungs, and other organs.

The damage happens quickly, even before the

short-lived high is over. The damage can also be permanent.[7]

Most chemicals are safe when properly used. They are tested repeatedly in laboratories. Everything from household cleaners to gasoline is carefully contained to reduce accidental exposure or inhalation. Still, accidents happen. In the 1970s, after the pesticide DDT was determined to be dangerous to wildlife, it was removed from the market. In the 1980s, a tragic chemical plant explosion in Bhopal, India, left thousands dead. Others died after Iraq's leader, Saddam Hussein, used chemical weapons on his own citizens.

Yet by the 1990s, most stories about dangerous chemicals did not involve environmental risk, accidental exposure, or even their use in warfare. The greatest concern was young people across the United States who routinely misused chemicals in their quest for a fleeting and often deadly high.

As the new century began, even as most teenage drug use declined, inhalant abuse exploded.

The National Inhalant Prevention Coalition explains that "Inhalants are chemicals that produce psychoactive (mind-altering) effects when abused or misused by concentrating and intentionally inhaling these fumes. These include volatile organic solvents, fuel gases, nitrates and anesthetic gases. Inhalants are volatile organic chemicals. Volatility is a measure of the [solvent's] tendency to vaporize or leave the liquid state."[8]

Inhalants are usually divided into four main categories:

1. Aliphatic nitrates. These are used predominantly by older teenagers and adults, and include amyl, butyl, and isobutyl nitrate. They are found in some room deodorizers and incense. Unlike other inhalants, these substances specifically increase the size of the blood vessels, acting primarily as a muscle relaxant.

The other three categories of inhalants affect the central nervous system.

2. Volatile solvents. Volatile solvents are liquids that vaporize at room temperature and include paint thinners, gasoline, nail polish remover, and lighter fluid. Felt-tip markers, correction fluid, model airplane glue, and computer cleaners also contain solvents.

3. Gases (which are invisible at room temperature) and propellants (compressed gas) include Freon and butane (found in disposable lighters). These substances are usually inhaled. Medical anesthetic gases include ether and chloroform, but the most common is nitrous oxide. Nitrous oxide, or "laughing gas," is often found in whipped cream containers abusers call "whippets." Sometimes this dangerous drug is sold at raves, all-night, all-ages dance parties where drugs are often used.

4. Aerosols. Aerosols usually come in a can. These sprays contain both propellants *and* solvents and include everything from deodorant to cooking sprays and spray paint.[9]

In the 1990s, drug tests became a fact of life for many teens participating in extracurricular activities or working part-time jobs. According to one medical report, part of the reason for inhalant's growing popularity was because they "cannot be detected by blood or urine tests."[10]

Recently, improved testing and better awareness by medical professionals who are trained to look for the signs of inhalant abuse

Aerosols contain propellants and solvents. Both are harmful if inhaled.

have yielded successful methods for detecting inhalants. In one, blood is tested using a method called gas chromatography. This reveals aliphatic hydrocarbons—the chemical signature for inhaled solvents.[11]

In addition to the other risks associated with inhalant abuse, users often restrict their oxygen supply, greatly increasing their chances for accidental asphyxiation. This occurs when an inhalant abuser breathes in dangerous chemicals, essentially crowding out the oxygen in the cells of the lungs. Without oxygen in the lungs, the victim is unable to breathe and death can occur quite quickly.

Some inhalant abusers get high from model airplane glue or spray paint. These products have one thing in common: toluene. This chemical solvent is quite effective when used properly. When inhaled, it can permanently damage the user's brain and nerve endings.

"Not all solvents bind to the same piece," notes Stephen Dewey, Ph.D., senior chemist at Brookhaven National Laboratory's Chemistry Department. Toluene does not bind to the white matter, but to the gray matter of the brain—a dopamine-rich area. This is the part of the reward system of the brain, the part that regulates the body's ability to feel joy or pleasure.[12]

Isolated inhalant abusers find themselves unable to feel joy or any pleasure at all when they are not getting high.

Toluene is not the only dangerous chemical inhalant abusers encounter. Studies done on long-term employees of chemical plants have proven how varied the damage can be.

Benzenes (found in paint thinners and inks) have been linked to leukemia and permanently destroy the body's immune system. Benzenes also affect bone marrow. This soft material within the bone cavity is the source of vital red blood cells.

Hexane (found in some glues) is responsible for the "stocking glove syndrome," where the feeling in the hands and fingers disappears.[13]

"When inhalant abusers inhale the toxic chemicals of common products," reports the National Inhalant Prevention Coalition, "the concentration of the fumes can be hundreds to thousands times greater than the maximum permitted in industrial settings."[14]

In the twenty-first century, manufacturing and chemical plants have developed a variety of ways to protect workers from the dangers of chemicals. Yet many teenagers voluntarily subject their bodies to the same risks.

For abusers of inhalants, the damage is frequently irreversible. Highs sought at age twelve or thirteen can affect the body and the mind for life.

In March 2004, guidelines developed by the Substance Abuse and Mental Health Administration were released. The guidelines hoped to improve the reporting of inhalant deaths by offering

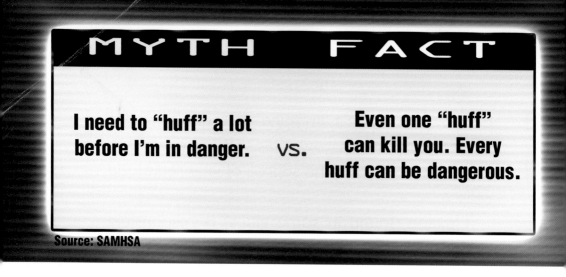

concrete information to medical examiners, coroners, and pathologists so they can determine cause of death.

The approximate one hundred deaths reported each year is considered to be far lower than the actual figure. Harvey Weiss, executive director of the National Inhalant Prevention Coalition, believes "information derived from outcomes of this tracking will be a valuable tool for evaluating prevention and treatment outcomes."[15]

In order to assess whether or not an unexplained death is related to inhalant abuse, investigators must look for clues. They examine faces stained by chemicals and sleeves soaked in paint thinner. They look for nails painted with correction fluid. A discarded plastic bag or rag might be discovered nearby. Sometimes empty containers of the chemical are found in the victim's room.

Unfortunately, autopsy findings do not always reveal the victim's history of inhalant abuse. Although fatty tissues can hold deposits of the chemicals for weeks, the most reliable methods test blood samples. Since many chemicals are not easily detected in standard examinations, specific tests are required to trace them and must be specially ordered. This only happens when there is an initial suspicion.[16] Often inhalant abusers take their secret to the grave.

CHAPTER THREE

INHALING HISTORY

Rising high above Greece's Gulf of Corinth, in the forested slopes of Mount Parnassus, the prophetess awaited inspiration. She was the Oracle of Delphi, a position handed down for generations. From 1200 B.C., until well into the fourth century, oracles advised Greek citizens. Marked by a large, cone-shaped rock and dedicated to Apollo, the god of prophecy, the temple was sacred ground for thousands who came for answers.

From commoners to kings, men and women traveled to this isolated outcropping of rocks and debris seeking advice about everything from love and money to warfare. After Socrates, the famous scholar and philosopher, visited the Oracle, she pronounced him the wisest man in the country. Alexander the Great sought the Oracle's predictions before important battles.

The Oracles altered history. They may also have been the world's best-known inhalant abusers.

The process for each Oracle was the same. A temple priest would bring her a question. The Oracle would then descend into a basement cell, inhaling deeply the fumes emanating from vents in the rocky floor. After entering a spastic, twitching trance, the Oracle answered the question.

The Oracles paid a heavy price for their "visions." There is some evidence that many died at a young age, or slipped into insanity. The connection between inhalant use and an early death was not as clear to the ancient Greeks as it is to today's researchers.

Long after the temple's destruction, when Roman emperor Julian the Apostate tried to restore its glory, the prophetess claimed her powers had disappeared.[1]

For centuries, the key to the Oracle's visions seemed to disappear as well.

Modern archaeologists were unable to find any evidence for the vents. The idea that the Oracles made their predictions because of chemicals was written off as a myth. Over twenty years ago, that began to change. In 1981, Dr. Jelle Zeilinga de Boer was working for the Greek government trying to find faults that could lead to earthquakes. East of the ancient temple site, a road had been recently widened. It was there that de Boer discovered a possible source for the Oracles' "advice."

"I had read Plutarch, and the Greek stories. And I started thinking, 'Hey, this could have been the fracture along which those fumes rose.'"[2]

He assumed others had already discovered it. He was wrong. In 1995, his description of the fault was met with skepticism. Dr. John R. Hale told de Boer that most archaeologists believed the fault was a legend.

Over the next three years, the pair explored

Archaeologists surveyed the land surrounding ancient ruins in Delphi looking for answers.

the area surrounding the Temple of Delphi, discovering both a second fault and an oily limestone deposit beneath the ground. Heated by what de Boer called "simple geologic actions," limestone can create petrochemical fumes, especially ethylene, which was used as a medical anesthetic during much of the twentieth century.

Testing the men's samples, Dr. Henry A. Spiller from the Kentucky Regional Poison Center explained, "There's a fair amount of data on the effects of ethylene. In the first stages it produces disembodied euphoria, an altered mental state and a pleasant sensation. It's what street people would call, 'getting high.' The greater the dose, the deeper you go."[3]

Around the same time period as the Delphi, passages in the Bible referred to the use of perfume in worship. The book *Licit and Illicit Drugs*, quoting from the fall 1967 *Journal of Addiction*, explains, "In the ancient Judaic world, the vapors from burnt spices and aromatic gums were considered part of a pleasurable act of worship . . ." Although it might seem like these ancient worshipers just enjoyed the sweet smells, the writers believed "in many or most cases, a psychoactive [mind-altering] drug was being inhaled."[4]

The practice of using "inhalants" as part of ceremonial rituals, from worship to predicting the future, has occurred across the planet for thousands of years.

In the 1800s, chemicals became more widely available due to both the beginning of modern medicine, which relied increasingly on various forms of anesthesia as part of surgeries, and the Industrial Revolution (where societies moved from economies based on farming to ones based on industry).

Chemicals used for surgery began as recreational drugs. Today, a trip to the dentist sometimes involves nitrous oxide, but the chemical's popularity began not with dental procedures, but with parties.

Discovered in 1772 by chemist Joseph Priestley, nitrous oxide was later synthesized by Sir Humphry Davy. Exposing nitrous peroxide to iron removed three of the four oxygen atoms, leaving a substance that produced in the user a heightened state of excitement, euphoria, and often the need to giggle uncontrollably, thus its nickname: "laughing gas."

Davy quickly added laughing gas to his parties. They were attended by some of the time's most interesting gentlemen, from potter Josiah Wedgwood (whose fine china is still sold today) to writer Peter Roget, future publisher of *Roget's Thesaurus*.[5]

As early as 1799, Davy suggested the chemical might be useful for medical procedures. Surgeries then were accompanied by perhaps a drink or two of whiskey, and nothing more. Despite the

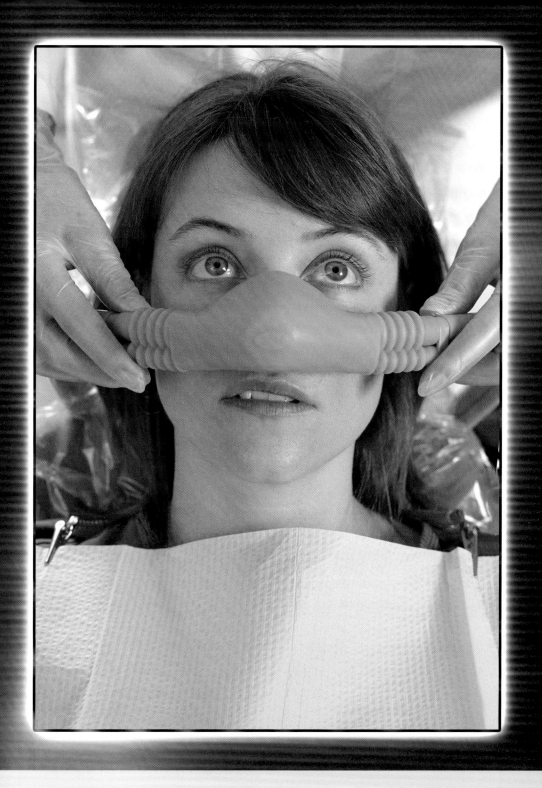

This woman receives nitrous oxide before a dental procedure.

advantages, nitrous oxide was not used medically for nearly half a century.

In the 1840s, medical student Gardner Quincy Colton decided to earn a little extra money for tuition. He acquired a few containers of nitrous oxide and had a party.

By then such parties were common. A notice from the era advertises, "Forty gallons of Gas will be prepared and administered to all in the audience who desire to inhale it. . . . Eight Young Men are engaged to occupy the front seats to protect those under influence of the Gas from injuring themselves or others. . . . The Gas will be administered only to gentleman of the first respectability. The object is to make the entertainment in every respect a genteel affair."[6]

MYTH		FACT
Inhalants are not addicting.	vs.	More and more young people are becoming addicted to inhalants, and when they quit they often suffer both physical and psychological withdrawal.

Colton's party was a success. After he was done paying for the gas and other expenses, he had five hundred dollars left over. At the time, that was more than he could have hoped to earn in a year as a doctor. The drug was legal and unregulated. Colton quit medical school and went into the party business full-time.

These parties were not all fun and games. Serious injuries were commonplace. Under the influence of the gas, revelers often fell or crashed into each other. The young men hired to protect the partygoers often failed at the job. In fact, it was an injury at a party that inspired a dentist to use anesthesia.

The dentist, Horace Wells, had watched horrified as a fellow reveler fell and gashed open his leg. The young dentist rushed to the man's side. Wells was astonished when the man told him he could not feel a thing.

Convinced nitrous oxide would eliminate pain in surgery, Wells decided to put it to the test. He became the first dental patient to be given gas before a procedure. Recruiting Colton to do the dentistry, Wells realized afterward how important the discovery was, exclaiming they were embarking on a "new era in tooth-pulling!"[7]

Top: Horace Wells. *Bottom*: Nitrous oxide and ether became common methods of anesthesia for dentistry and surgery.

It took some time before "pain-free dentistry" caught on. Wells's efforts were ridiculed by his fellow dentists, especially after one hapless patient began screaming in agony when the gas was too low and the pain kicked in. Still, the use of nitrous oxide in surgeries slowly gained popularity.

Today, it is difficult to imagine a time when a tooth could be pulled or a cavity filled without anesthesia.

Another anesthesia, ether, followed a similar course. It, too, was used first in recreation. In the 1840s, Harvard University was famous for "ether parties." Ether was also added to alcohol during Prohibition in the 1920s, when liquor was illegal and often homemade. The added ether was thought to improve its intoxicating power. Unfortunately, it also made it more dangerous. Like nitrous oxide, ether was adopted as an anesthetic and was used in surgeries until well into the twentieth century.

In the United States, inhalant abuse began to be a problem during World War II when some soldiers huffed gasoline after soaking it into a rag. Building plastic model airplanes became a popular hobby after the war. Their assembly required the use of a specific glue that contained the chemical

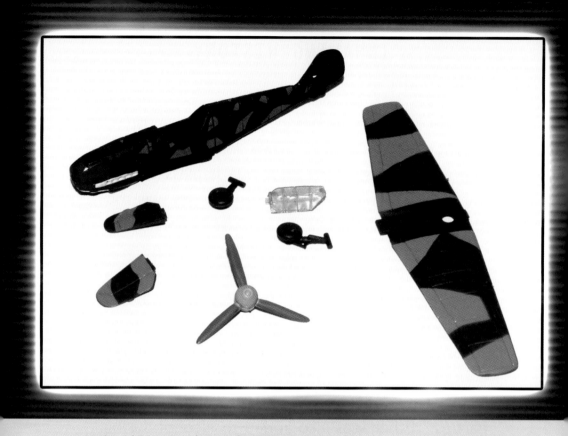

In the 1950s, the abuse of model airplane glue was a growing concern.

toluene. When inhaled, this substance produces a light-headed euphoria. Perhaps the first idea of its effects came from building a model in a room with the windows shut (model airplane glue, like most chemicals, should only be used in a well-ventilated space).

By the end of the 1950s, recreational use of airplane glue was a national concern. The practice spread to beat poets, the usually dark-garbed coffeehouse customers known for their love of jazz, radical poetry and drugs. Later on, students protesting the Vietnam War, sometimes called hippies, described inhaling glue as similar to, but faster acting than, alcohol. Most of them used it along with other drugs, like marijuana and liquor, but the glue was probably the most dangerous.

In South American countries, such as Brazil and Honduras, huffing has become epidemic. Unlike the United States, its use is confined mainly to children from very poor families. Many abusers are "street kids," either orphaned or cut off from their parents, and some are younger than ten years old. They abuse inhalants as a means of coping with their hunger and the cold.

In India, one recent medical journal article points out that "inhalant users coming to [rehab] clinics are predominantly socio-economically deprived young males aged 10–18," and worries that "inhalant abuse is becoming a significant public health problem in India, more so due to the lack of awareness among the general population and even the health professionals regarding the abuse potential and consequences."[8]

From ether parties in the nineteenth century to new millennium preteens experimenting with chemicals, the search for a cheap high has

This man (background) sniffs glue outside a restaurant in Honduras.

continued. There is no way to keep every dangerous substance away from those who would abuse it. Although the Oracles of Delphi might have claimed visions, they lacked the benefit of information and education: the best way to prevent needless death and injury. With better access to more information than any generation in history, today's young adults can quickly learn the truth about how deadly these short-lived highs really are.

CHAPTER FOUR

SNIFFING DEATH

More than any other drug abuser, those who use inhalants are rarely suspected —not by their teachers or friends, and not even by their parents. "Only three percent of parents think their child has ever abused inhalants," explains Stephen J. Pasierb, president of the Partnership for a Drug-Free America.[1]

Two years ago, Johnson Bryant was on the honor roll. He was an athlete. He attended an elite private school.

Last year, Bryant died.

"It's frightening to see your son in a body bag," his mother, Toy Bryant, recalled. "When the coroner said it looked like he'd inhaled butane, I thought, 'This is something I see on [television news shows]. . . . There is no pain like losing a child . . . Some mornings I can't get out of bed."[2]

"Inhalant abuse is the most hidden of all drug problems," admits University of Texas Gulf Coast Addiction Center researcher Jane C. Maxwell, Ph.D.[3] Many parents don't know their child is abusing inhalants.

One reason is that parents who went to high school in the 1970s abused drugs at a higher rate than any other group before or since. For some, these drug experiences as teenagers make them less likely to talk to their own kids about drug abuse. "Parents who are not communicating to their kids, and kids who don't perceive the risk of inhalants, is a recipe for disaster," Pasierb explains.[4]

Most drug use is reduced by the risks of

possession. Although locker searches might turn up illegal drugs, teens can buy cooking spray or nail polish remover without suspicion. Not every potentially dangerous substance can be made illegal just because someone might misuse it.

Many in law enforcement believe a better awareness by parents and peers can reduce this problem. Possession is not the best giveaway, behavior is.

Because the substances used by inhalant abusers are so commonplace, witnesses to behavior are often the best way of getting them help. Although friends might be concerned about "snitching out" their peers, inhalant abusers put their life on the line every time they get high.

Even if they do not overdose, one medical journal notes that "young people who use inhalants heavily may not learn how to solve problems, handle their emotions and become mature, responsible adults."[5]

Damage from inhalant abuse is a heavy burden for a teen to carry into adulthood. It is vital to know the signs of inhalant abuse. The symptoms of inhalant abuse are as varied as the chemicals that are abused. Despite this variety, there are common signs to look for.

INHALANTS = BUSTED!

Like other drugs, the first sign of abuse is often the drug itself. While most of the substances with a potential for abuse have innocent uses, finding discarded empties of things like cooking spray or hair spray, or rags soaked in chemicals like gasoline, can be a giveaway. So, too, can the discovery of several half-used or empty tubes of modeling glue, bottles of correction fluid, or nail polish remover.

Regular inhalant abusers may have a distinctive smell. Their breath, even their skin, can give off a sweet, chemical odor. Solvents like paint thinner can stain their mouth or their hands.

There are physical symptoms as well. Users may have a lack of appetite; many inhalant abusers lose weight. Kids who sniff markers can be identified by the colored marks left on their nose. Witnessing someone regularly sniffing their sleeve may indicate that they have been soaking them in a chemical to get high. From irritability to sudden mood changes, there are numerous signs others can watch for. The key is to be observant.

A thirteen-year-old girl visited her family doctor after complaining of headaches. Her mother said "she was not eating much" and was often clumsy. The girl had dry, cracked skin, sores on her mouth, and her fingernails were stained with ink. In private she admitted to sniffing paint and glue. If not for her mother's careful observation, her abuse might have been ignored. Instead, a potentially deadly habit was ended.[6]

Along with these symptoms, some abusers may be pale or appear sickly. They sometimes complain of a persistent cold lasting for weeks; this "illness" gives them an excuse to miss school. They skip to get high.

Besides their appearance, inhalant abusers often act "drunk"—slurring their words, giggling, and falling easily. They may become hyperactive, nervous, or easily upset. They can have physical reactions, such as nausea and vomiting, to the chemicals they are using. Some inhalant abusers become paranoid, believing others are following them or want to do them harm. This can even make them distrust their best friends. Still, friends can be the best solution, especially if the abuser is not comfortable confiding in an adult. Adults might ignore a teen who is depressed or anti-social, figuring it is normal adolescent behavior.

In 2002 and 2003, an annual average of 718,000 youths aged 12 or 13 had used an inhalant in their lifetime.

Source: SAMHSA

Peers can have a better understanding of what normal teenage emotions are.

Besides the emotional damage done by inhalant abuse, there are very real physical dangers. Even one "experiment" can kill.

"Research has found that even a single session of repeated inhalant abuse can disrupt heart rhythms and cause death from cardiac arrest or lower oxygen levels enough to cause suffocation," explains Nora Volkow, director of the National Institute on Drug Abuse.[7]

"The debilitating and potentially lethal effects of inhalants can occur even with first use. Sudden sniffing death syndrome is usually caused by the irregular heart rate induced by inhalants; other cardiac effects are hypertension, tachycardia, and bradycardia. Other significant effects include command seizures. Brain damage can be a consequence of chronic use."[8] Hypertension is high blood pressure, tachycardia is rapid heartbeat; bradycardia is abnormally slow heartbeat. Death occurs from cardiac arrest: a heart attack.

Butane, propane, Freon, and "poppers" are all connected to sudden sniffing death syndrome. Poppers is a slang term for various alkyl nitrates. Alkyl nitrates were once prescribed as capsules to heart patients. The capsules were broken, or "popped," to release vapors. Flammable liquids like gasoline and butane carry the added risk that a single spark might ignite, causing burn injuries.

Inhaling petroleum products, like propane and gasoline, damages the lungs, and coolants like Freon injure the airways just like frostbite injures the skin. Nitrous oxide and the plastic bags favored by some inhalant abusers cause suffocation.

Despite the possibility of dying from one experiment with inhalants, the Partnership for a Drug-Free America reported that "between 2001 and 2003, the number of eighth graders who agreed with the statement that 'sniffing or huffing things to get high can kill you,' fell from 73 % to 63 %. Among sixth graders, the number fell from 68 % in 2001 to 48 % in 2003."[9]

The gradual decline among eighth-graders since 2001 in the perceived risk of using inhalants continued from 2003 to 2004.[10]

The omnipresent threat of overdosing on inhalants and dying is not the only risk. In a study done of 847 adolescents admitted to a drug treatment facility, researchers noticed a surprising thing. "The lifetime prevalence of depression

Some teens may turn to inhalants in order to relieve their depression. If you are depressed or know someone who may be depressed, talk to an adult you trust.

increased with the severity of inhalant involvement and nearly 40% of adolescents with inhalant abuse or dependence in our sample met criteria for lifetime diagnosis of major depression." Since this is based on self-reporting (patients describing their own depression) rather than clinical data from therapy, researchers believe this number may be higher. The reason the actual number is so surprising is that previous studies have not found a link between depression and inhalant abuse.

This one did. In fact, the study went on to say that "our data support that adolescents who use inhalants or have an inhalant use disorder are at high risk of reporting symptoms of major depression."[11]

According to one Duke University professor, "During adolescence, brain organization and function enter a unique period of flux [change]." The frontal lobe portion of the brain, responsible for decision making and impulse control, along with other vital functions, undergoes profound changes. The so-called gray matter is "pruned" as myelin cells increase while unnecessary synapse functions decrease. This peaks at about age sixteen or seventeen. Meanwhile, dopamine receptors (which help regulate mood) increase in size. These changes in the brain along with the stresses of growing up in twenty-first-century America, mean many teens struggle with depression, mood swings, and anxiety.[12]

As medical director for Child and Adolescent Psychiatry at Legacy Emmanuel Hospital in Portland, Oregon, Dr. Ken Ensroth has seen the number of teens and preteens abusing inhalants increase in the last decade. Many of those admitted to rehabilitation programs at this hospital may use inhalants because, "like some other drugs, inhalants are dulling—they could take them for anxiety."[13]

In their study of 847 people, the researchers noted how, in adults, substance-induced depression rarely lasts for more than a month, but "in adolescents with substance use disorders, depressive disorders do not remit with abstinence."[14] In other words, stopping inhalants does not end the depression.

Research suggests that about one in four inhalant abusers attempts suicide at some point during his or her addiction.[15]

Entering adolescence, young people experience radical shifts in how their brain produces dopamine. This chemical is responsible for mood regulation. Lower levels of dopamine are linked to depression, anxiety, and aggressive behavior. This shift is partly why many teenagers endure dramatic mood swings.

Dopamine can be increased by a variety of factors. Exercising, receiving a compliment, or even falling in love can increase dopamine. Unfortunately, some adolescents turn to chemicals. Drugs like MDMA (ecstasy), cocaine, and alcohol all have radical impacts on dopamine

This memorial was dedicated to five girls that died in a car accident. Four of the five girls were found to have traces of the inhalant difluoroethane in their blood.

production. Whenever dopamine is artificially increased, there is a corresponding decrease; what goes up must eventually come down, including moods.

Inhalants increase dopamine production quite quickly, and also have a subsequent reduction in mood. This "inhalant onset depressive episode" can make the highs and lows of normal teenage "mood swings" into a much more damaging condition. Sometimes it even resembles mental illness or bipolar disorder.[16]

In tests done on long-term inhalant abusers, the destruction was obvious and not surprising. Inhaling chemicals repeatedly for months and years on end damages an abuser's brain. Some inhalant abusers could not concentrate or focus. They had difficulty remembering material for tests. More severe impairments were also discovered. Some were permanently unable to recall information, despite quitting inhalant abuse years before the studies.

In early studies conducted in the 1960s and 1970s, researchers broke down the characteristics of inhalant abusers. As reported by the National Inhalant Prevention Coalition, these characteristics were divided into stages depending on the amount and frequency of the abuse.

Adolescents who begin experimenting with chemical highs can expect to pass through these stages. There is not a set amount of time for how quickly this occurs. However, since young adults are still maturing physically, usually their progression occurs more rapidly than it does with older people.

Immediately after inhaling, the user enters Stage One: the Excitatory Stage. This is marked by a range of symptoms, including euphoria, excitation, sneezing, coughing, light intolerance, nausea, and vomiting. Sometimes in this stage the user experiences hallucinations and their skin is flushed and hot.

Stage Two is referred to as Early Central Nervous System Depression. In this stage, the user might experience confusion, his body feels numb, and his surroundings seem less interesting as he retreats inside himself. A user may hear a buzzing or ringing in his ears, experience blurred or double vision, cramps, headaches, or insensitivity to pain; and have an increased paleness of the skin.

Stage Three, or Medium Central Nervous System Depression, is where the chemical abuser first experiences drowsiness, lack of muscular coordination, slurred speech, depressed reflexes, and the rapid involuntarily movement of the eyeballs.

Stage Four is the Late Central Nervous System Depression, which includes unconsciousness accompanied by bizarre dreams and seizures.

Hallucinations are far more common in inhalant abusers than in alcohol abusers.[17]

The best way to stay safe is not to start. But what about the friend of the inhalant abuser? It is not easy to be the nonusing friend of an inhalant abuser. Just when the abuser needs them the most, friends are driven away. For inhalant abusers, friends might be their only hope.

Unlike many other drugs, getting caught is less of a risk. Substances like nail polish remover or model airplane glue may have innocent explanations, and as one medical report explains, "They do not produce red eyes or other signs of intoxication. They act only for a short time."[18]

Lowered inhibitions that accompany all drug abuse can lead to other severe consequences, including sexual assaults and fighting. Teens experimenting with chemicals may suddenly become angry—even violently so. Andrew Sandy's mother complained about his outbursts, and he even threatened a teacher.[19] "Inhalant abusers experience higher drop out and expulsion rates than any other type of drug abuser," says the National Inhalant Prevention Coalition, "because they are often erratic, uncooperative and exhibit violent

Inhaled chemicals, and many other drugs, may cause people to lash out at friends and family for no reason.

behaviors."[20] They are also more likely to be arrested.

Like other drugs, inhalants change motivated and focused students into disinterested ones. Relationships with family members and nonusing peers deteriorate.

According to the National Inhalant Prevention Coalition, doctors Neil Rosenberg and Charles Sharp have identified four main categories of inhalant abusers: The "transient social user" has not used for very long and uses with friends. He or she is usually ten to sixteen years old. However, the "chronic social user" usually is in his or her twenties and has been using inhalants for over five years. This person still uses primarily with friends but exhibits brain damage, has probably dropped out of high school, and has been arrested at least once. The "transient isolate user" does the drug alone only occasionally and tends to be ten to sixteen years old. By contrast, the "chronic isolate user" is in his or her twenties and, besides poor social skills, also has an arrest record and a limited education.[21]

Having an idea of the physical characteristics of inhalant abuse is one of the best ways to help the occasional experimenter from moving to regular and debilitating use.

Suspicions of drug use should be discussed with a helpful adult, a teacher, or a parent. Confronting the abuser usually provokes denial. Even if he or she admits to trying a substance to get high, he or she may describe it as "an experiment."

Deciding whether or not the individual use was a "one-time thing" or a pattern of behavior is best left to treatment professionals. John Mitchell runs a substance abuse program in Maryland and says that upon seeing potential abusers, most treatment professionals are very precise in detailing a patient's level of drug use.[22]

One-time experimentation does not mean the user will wind up in a locked-down rehabilitation facility. In the case of Mitchell's program, the user might be steered to a three-month educational program. Regardless of the outcome, intensive rehabilitation or an educational program, help must be found for recreational inhalant users.

Although alcohol and inhalants share similar symptoms (some huffers call their abuse a "cheap drunk"), there is a crucial difference. The difference lies in the body processes. About 20 percent of alcohol (like anything swallowed) is absorbed in the stomach; the rest is absorbed in the small intestine. Only after absorption does the alcohol enter the bloodstream before dissolving in the water of the body tissue (except for fat tissue, which cannot absorb alcohol). Once dissolved in the tissues, the alcohol begins to affect the entire body. It can take half an hour or more before the full effects of a single drink are felt.[23]

While this "delayed reaction" leads many to become more intoxicated than they intended, there is no such delay when someone is abusing inhalants. It is possible to become impaired almost immediately.

This is because the way the body processes inhaled chemicals is quite similar to the way it processes crack cocaine. Anything smoked and inhaled (through the mouth or the nose) goes immediately to the lungs. The lungs are partly responsible for the movement of oxygenated blood, which is quite efficient at transporting anything that comes into them quickly.

"Organic solvents are highly lipophilic, or highly attracted to the fatty tissue on the body," explains the National Inhalant Prevention Coalition. "This means that they are more soluble in fats than in water. Therefore solvents will readily leave the blood and quickly accumulate in the fat cells of the brain, heart, liver and muscles and remain there for a considerable period of time. The central and peripheral nervous system, liver, kidneys, lungs, heart and adrenal gland will have a highly toxic chemical content even after a single inhalation. Because of concentration of these toxins in the body of a chronic abuser, detoxification of solvents from the body can take several weeks."[24] Inhalant abusers get high very quickly; usually the level of intoxication is far greater than anticipated. The user quickly loses control. The price he or she pays can last a lifetime.

CHAPTER FIVE

HUFFING TOWARD DISASTER

Perhaps more than the potential damage to the body, it is the permanent damage to the brain that should deter potential inhalant abusers. The damage is well known in the medical community. Doctors often treat kids who experiment with inhalants and suffer from "memory loss, especially short-term memory loss [forgetting something you were told a few minutes before], delusions or hallucinations; slurred or changed speech, staggering, stumbling."[1]

Fourteen-year-old Megan Hakeman was out of control. Joyriding atop a friend's car, she fell off, winding up with a nasty concussion. She was high at the time. But then, at that time in her life, she was almost always high. So much so that her best friend just stopped speaking to her. When she was home, she would fight with her brother, or her mother. In those arguments, she later admitted, "I always hit my mom when I was using."[2]

When sixteen-year-old Megan spoke about her experiences in 2003, she had not huffed in nearly two years. Her path to drug addiction began when she was twelve as a way to escape a personal trauma. In the end, it cost her her friends and very nearly her life. Yet even after almost twenty-four months of sobriety, Megan had lost something she might never get back: her memory.

"I can't really remember a lot of things. When I'm talking, I'll forget what I said just two seconds ago. It frustrates me a lot."[3]

The problem is that the chemicals are so

dangerous, often it is hard for others to believe teens would even experiment with them. Despite the numerous risks of other substances, such as marijuana or alcohol, every time a person uses inhalants he or she is literally inhaling poisons. Or as Dr. Ken Ensroth puts it, "Medical staff, anyone who is reasonably well educated, realizes that it's really freaky-bad putting this toxic stuff into your body."[4]

Medical professionals have a difficult time understanding why many young adults abuse inhalants, while parents have an even tougher time accepting it. Studies consistently show only a tiny percentage of parents suspect their children might be experimenting with inhalants. "Parents are talking less about it. Little happens unless people recognize the problem," explains Harvey Weiss, founder of the National Inhalant Prevention Coalition.[5]

Beginning in the late 1990s, medical reports explained that huffing is the most common form of substance abuse among school-age and preadolescent children (ages eight to twelve).[6]

What increases the challenge is that, unlike other drugs, inhalants are more often used by those in the middle grades (from fourth through eighth grade) than by older adolescents. "It's more easily accessible, teens are more mobile and likely have some money—younger kids don't as easily," Ensroth explains.[7]

Inhalant abusers may have some level of trauma in their lives, from abuse to foster care. Because of this they often do not have the same level of family support their friends have.[8]

Still, some studies suggest inhalant-abusing teens are no more likely to come from homes where the parents are not well educated. Trends suggest family income and education may not be as large a factor in determining whether or not a young adult uses inhalants.[9]

Instead, it is more a matter of unsupervised time, and a disconnection among most of their peers. "Young inhalant users tend to be more alienated than other youth," explains the National Inhalant Prevention Coalition Web site. "These feelings of alienation may be important factors leading a young person to find other alienated youth which may then lead to inhalant abuse."[10]

Although these kids often use inhalants socially, their use actually further isolates them socially. That is because the inhalant abuser might have a tight group of other users, but nonusers shun them. Because they are isolated from most of their classmates, their only "friends" are users.

A nonusing acquaintance has to make the first move to help an inhalant abuser. Peers are in a good position to do something. They can be the best ones to notice changes in attitude or behavior. These changes can be related to many things, but talking to the person at risk can really make a difference.

Inhaling chemicals or abusing other drugs is not an answer. Find nonusing friends that you can hang out with.

Often parents and teachers have never seen an abuser under the influence. Peers might witness the warning signs, from the abuser having a distinct chemical smell to acting "drunk." Even a casual acquaintance may realize something is wrong.

Drug abusers might be reluctant to discuss their behavior but even "at ten or eleven years old, they are old enough to do peer-to-peer confrontation," explains Ensroth. He says confronters should say something like, "'What are you doing?' Ask them about it, go to an adult involved, say something about them and your concern."[11]

If the friend is not interested in discussing the problem, talking about it with a parent or teacher is crucial. "Don't just push it away and think it's not a problem," Ensroth says. "If you have a worry about it, better safe than sorry. If you're wrong, no harm done. If you're right and you help them get help, it's a good thing."[12]

On the opposite side, as a way of preventing inhalant abuse, William D. Crano, Ph.D., a professor at the School of Behavioral and Organizational Science at Claremont Graduate University, has an idea. "Maybe we should stress peer disapproval.

Peer opinion matters to eleven to twelve year olds."[13]

Disapproval in general, coupled with confrontation and one-on-one discussions, might be the most important strategy. A casual user can become a chronic user; inhalant abuse peaks around eighth grade. By high school, inhalant abuse is not just disliked, it is often considered a sign of immaturity. "Inhalant use tends to begin and end at an early age," explains Lloyd Johnson, who oversees the Monitoring the Future survey. "It's seen as a kid's drug."[14]

It is important to reach the user early and reinforce that despite its growing popularity, it remains a drug that is done by very few. Inhalant abusers exaggerate how many of their peers do

MYTH		FACT
It is not like other, illegal drugs.	VS.	Researchers believe inhalants are a common "gateway drug"; their use leads to other drugs. Besides, inhaling chemicals to get high is illegal!

the drug; less than twenty out of every one hundred eighth graders have ever experimented with these deadly chemicals. Still, in 2005, drug abuse professionals noted that one "surprising trend among use of inhalants is that, among eighth graders, inhalant abuse by girls exceeds use by boys."[15]

Girls, like boys, abuse a variety of products, but for many of them their drug of choice is the one they use most often, the one they can carry without suspicion. "Nail polish remover," notes Ensroth, "they sniff it once, like the high, and keep doing it."[16] A solvent, nail polish remover contains acetone.

If peers, parents, doctors, or teachers do not notice, the downward spiral continues. Most drug-using young adults are admitted to rehabilitation and recovery programs because of an arrest. Inhalant abusers often abuse other drugs as well, reports researcher Li-Tzy Wu, who explains that "Our study provides more evidence that early use of inhalants may be a precursor for later drug abuse that grows to include abuse of multiple illegal substances."[17]

Possessing other illegal drugs is more likely to lead to the abuser's arrest. The user begins treatment and recovery under a court order. Unfortunately, many inhalant abusers are never caught.

The first known law against "sniffing glue" was passed in Anaheim, California, in 1962. Some laws related to graffiti also affected inhalant abusers because they restricted possession of substances like spray paint. Recently, large home improvement stores have implemented systems similar to the ones used to restrict the sales of alcohol to minors. When certain products are rung up at the cash register, the clerk is required to check for proof of age before completing the sale.

While most stores only follow this procedure in the thirty states where sales to minors of potential inhalants are illegal, in May 2003, Lowes home improvement stores implemented such a policy nationwide. Over twelve hundred products were flagged for proof-of-age checks—from paint thinner to cleaning products.[18]

However, no amount of regulation can reduce inhalant abuse among teens and preteens intent upon getting high. The products are too widely available.

"This is a demand reduction issue, not a supply issue," Robert Balster, Ph.D., explained at a 2005

How Can You Tell If a Friend Is Using Inhalants?

If your friend has one or more of the following warning signs, he or she may be using inhalants:

- Slurred speech
- Drunk, dizzy, or dazed appearance
- Unusual breath odor
- Chemical smell on clothing
- Paint stains on body or face
- Red eyes
- Runny nose

Source: SAMHSA

Anti-Drug Conference. The professor at Virginia Commonwealth University and director of the Institute for Drug and Alcohol Studies said that "Elimination of products is improbable."[19]

The best way to not get addicted is not to start, but for those who have begun abusing inhalants, new hope is emerging.

CHAPTER SIX

NEW HOPE

"I was thirteen, maybe fourteen years old," Courtney told a reporter, recalling the first time she abused inhalants. "I didn't think it was dangerous at all. I thought it was not nearly as bad as using drugs because everybody else was doing it. It can't be that bad—the stuff is just lying around the classroom—or the house—so I thought. It's not like I was getting something from a drug dealer."[1]

Courtney greatly underestimated the dangers. For her—and many other young teens—inhalants were the first step toward abusing other drugs. By the time she was old enough to drive, she was also addicted to heroin while still abusing inhalants. She underwent months of intensive drug treatment, and even after becoming "clean and sober," she still suffers memory lapses and has difficulty concentrating. Courtney's counselor at the Pathway Family Center, Victoria Winebarger, explains that inhalant abusers can suffer unique and permanent consequences. "I've seen kids that have had severe brain damage from inhalants," she explained, "damage that has impaired their memory and balance."[2]

People who are addicted to alcohol and want to get better go to Alcoholics Anonymous (AA). Kids with alcoholic parents might opt for Alateen. Cocaine addicts might go to Cocaine Anonymous (CA); Marijuana addicts go to Marijuana Anonymous (MA). "There are less clear treatment protocols for inhalant abuse," admits psychiatrist Dr. Ken Ensroth. "Alcohol has pretty clear detox procedures. Alcohol and narcotics have twelve-step meetings."[3]

Begun in the 1930s, Alcoholics Anonymous was founded to provide a supportive program for people who wanted to stop drinking. Before AA, most people saw alcoholics as "drunks," weak people who drank because they lacked the will power or desire to quit. It was seen as a behavior problem. AA helped popularize the growing belief in the medical community that alcoholism was a disease.[4]

Today, millions worldwide attend AA meetings. Even more importantly, its famous twelve steps for recovery have been incorporated in numerous other recovery programs from CA and MA to those used in rehabilitation centers.

Recovery begins for an addict when he or she accepts that the problem is not one he or she has physical power over and that just wanting to stop is not enough (although an important part of the process).

Despite the rising trend in inhalant abuse, many rehab directors do not report a corresponding increase in admissions to their programs. One director, John Mitchell, thinks he knows why. "Just because the numbers in rehab programs

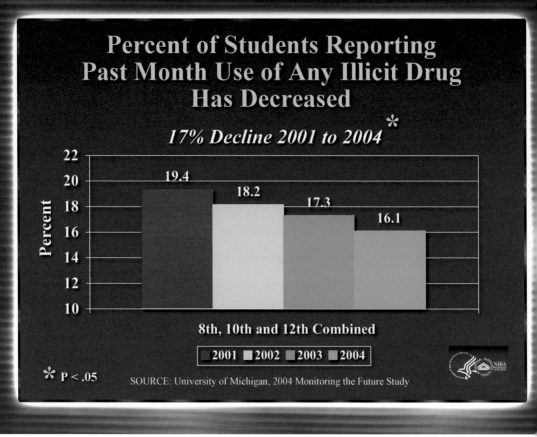

Percent of Students Reporting Past Month Use of Any Illicit Drug Has Decreased

17% Decline 2001 to 2004 *

8th, 10th and 12th Combined

2001 ■ 2002 ■ 2003 ■ 2004

19.4   18.2   17.3   16.1

* P < .05   SOURCE: University of Michigan, 2004 Monitoring the Future Study

haven't gone up doesn't mean the number of kids using hasn't gone up," explains Mitchell. "Instead, many users—especially inhalant users—could be part of a hidden population, drug abusers who aren't arrested, aren't discovered by schools or parents but continue to abuse."[5]

Just as challenging is the fact that while most admissions for other drugs are in their middle teens or older, inhalant abusers can be younger, some as young as ten. "We have not geared our program to kids that age in the past," admits Mitchell, "but we have tried to adapt."[6]

In fact, not very long ago, because of inhalant abusers' unique problems, "many treatment facilities refused to treat inhalant abusers, judging them to be 'resistant to treatment,'" according to the National Inhalant Prevention Coalition.[7]

Only recently has that begun to change. But even as programs adapt to the growing wave of inhalant abusers, rehabilitation professionals admit that addicts present unique challenges for recovery.

"Volatile substance abusers are among the most difficult," explains one report. "The research on background and psychosocial characteristics show this group to typically have serious, multiple problems that lead to dysfunction in a wide range of social and personal contexts. Most treatment programs are not equipped to deal with the intensity of problems that solvent abusers present."[8]

At his program, Dr. Ensroth finds that it is necessary to look at inhalant abuse as different from other forms of drug abuse. "Yes, it's a drug abuse problem," explains Ensroth, "but it's very off—out of line. . . . I look for other problems in their judgment, problems in their thinking: bipolar or psychotic illness. It seems so clear, the sense that it's bad for you."[9]

At Mitchell's program, like those across the country, the treatment professional gauges the level of abuse, determines if there is "cross addiction" (the abuse of other substances in addition to inhalants), and studies the user's psychology. The patient is screened for possible underlying mental health problems—like anxiety or depression. Drug tests are done to get a baseline, or an idea of what substances are in the user's system when he or she begins treatment.

Screening for inhalant abuse must be very specific. Asking if the subject has sniffed a drug might get a negative response if he or she is think-ing of cocaine or methamphetamine, for example. Many who abuse other drugs may ignore their inhalant addiction.

Depending on the level of abuse, some patients may qualify for outpatient treatment. A normal, level-one client at Mitchell's program would receive three to nine hours of peer-to-group counseling and one-on-one counseling, along with drug testing about once a week. An intensive, level-two client would have more fre-quent drug testing and over nine hours a week of peer-to-group and one-on-one sessions. Like many small counties, Calvert County, Maryland, does not have an inpatient drug treatment program.

Whether inpatient or outpatient, programs work with the inhalant abuser's parents or guardians to ensure that chemicals with a potential for abuse are removed from their home.[10]

When first admitted to an inpatient facility, the user begins a process of withdrawal. The withdrawal symptoms usually begin within a day or two after the abuser's last use and often last for nearly a week. They include sleep disturbances, tremors, irritability, dry mouth, nausea, and even hallucinations.[11]

Withdrawal is just the first hurdle. Even after the dangerous chemicals have been purged from an abuser's system, the drug's influence remains. The user wants to use again.

Detoxification of the dangerous chemicals and treatment for drug dependency can be a lengthy process. Part of the challenge is that the inhalants have often altered the patient's ability to concentrate or listen to others. Patients have difficulty adjusting to therapy; it is recommended that counseling sessions in the early stages of treatment not last for more than twenty minutes.

The problems an inhalant abuser may be

experiencing mentally, along with the detox procedures, leads experts to advise far longer inpatient programs. With most drugs, inpatient stays of between fourteen to twenty-eight days are standard. Inhalant abusers are often in inpatient programs for ninety days or more. The stay is sometimes extended to 120 days.[12]

Recently, scientists applying what they have learned treating addictions to heroin and nicotine (which is found in tobacco) made a surprising discovery with the drug Vigabratin (also known as gamma-vinyl-GABA or GVG), which has been used to treat these addictions. In 2004, scientists at the Brookhaven National Laboratory trained rats to expect toluene vapors in a certain location. The rats became addicted to the toluene (which is commonly found in products like airplane glue). After randomly administering either saline or GVG to the rats, the rats were then allowed to go to the spot where they had come to expect the toluene vapors. This time the toluene was not released; the rats with just saline searched frantically, spending over five minutes trying to find toluene. Rats who had received GVG gave up their quest in less than ninety seconds.[13]

"The findings of this study extend the potential value of GVG to treat addiction," explains Brookhaven researcher Stephen Dewey. "More importantly, our results show promise in treating inhalant abuse as it continues to grow as a problem among adolescents."[14]

Treating chemical addiction with another chemical is controversial. Treatment professionals agree that the growing problem of inhalant abuse must be discussed further so fewer kids will be tempted to experiment with such deadly chemicals.

"It may be time for a new ad campaign, among other things," says Lloyd Johnson, Ph.D., who has seen inhalant abuse grow among young people. "It's time for the field to mobilize."[15]

John Mitchell understands what is needed: "I think the important thing is to get to kids at a younger age and parents earlier—not to scare people but to educate them. If we don't do it, who knows what the consequences will be."[16]

By getting the best information about why dangerous highs should be avoided, young adults can make a difference and avoid possibly fatal consequences.

GLOSSARY

anesthetic—A chemical, such as ether or nitrous oxide, that causes loss of sensation, either local numbing or unconsciousness. Used in surgery.

bipolar disorder—Mental illness marked by distinctly depressive and manic behaviors.

central nervous system—The connected system of the brain and spinal cord.

cerebellum—Part of the brain that controls voluntary muscular movement.

cerebral cortex—Outer layer of gray tissue in the brain responsible for coordination of sensory and motor information.

dopamine—Neurotransmitter found in the regions of the brain that regulate movement, pleasure, and emotion.

epidemiology—Study of the factors controlling the absence or presence of a disease or other health condition.

psychoactive—Having the ability to affect the mind or behavior. Usually applied to a chemical agent or drug.

psychotic—Person suffering from mental illness marked by withdrawal from reality and a severe decline in social functioning.

toxic—Poisonous. Or a substance that, when introduced into the body, can harm the functioning of an organ or group of organs, including the heart, lungs, and brain.

withdrawal—Variety of painful symptoms that occur after use of addictive drug is reduced or stopped.

CHAPTER NOTES

Chapter 1. Deadly Games

1. Michael Amon, "'Huffing' Blamed in Teen's Death," *Washington Post*, March 22, 2002, p. B5.
2. Personal interview with John Mitchell, director of Calvert County Substance Abuse Services, January 26, 2005.
3. Amon, p. B5.
4. Mary Ellen Schneider, "Effort aims to improve data on inhalant deaths," *Family Practice News*, June 1, 2004, v. 34, issue 11, p. 55.
5. "New Findings on Inhalants: Parent and Youth Attitudes," *The Partnership for a Drug-Free America*, n.d., <http://www.drugfree.org/Portal/ DrugIssue/News/New_Findings_on_Inhalants_ Parent_and_Youth> (March 16, 2005).
6. Amon, p. B5.
7. Robert P. Giovacchini, "An Industrial/ Economic Perspective of Inhalant Abuse," *National Institute on Drug Abuse Research Monograph 129, Inhalant Abuse: A Volatile Research Agenda*, 1992, pp. 276–277.
8. "Teen Drug Use Declines 2003–2004, But Concerns Remain About Inhalants and Pain Killers," *National Institute on Drug Abuse*, n.d., <http://www.drugabuse.gov/Newsroom/04/ NR12-21.html> (December 21, 2004).
9. Ibid.

10. "Inhalant Abuse; New Research Identifies Factors Related to Inhalant Abuse, Addiction," *Women's Health Weekly*, October 28, 2004, p. 93.

Chapter 2. Toxic Chem Lab

1. Laura D. Angelo, "A Young Huffer's Heartbreak," *Scholastic Choices*, vol. 15, no. 5, February 1, 2000, p. 16.

2. Sarah Maclean, "It might be a scummy-arsed drug but it's a sick buzz," *Contemporary Drug Problems*, vol. 32, no. 2, July 1, 2005, p. 295.

3. Cate Baily, "Inhalants—Pain Meets Poison," *Science World*, vol. 59, no. 11, March 7, 2003, p. 20.

4. "Research Report Series—Inhalant Abuse: What Are Inhalants?" *National Institute on Drug Abuse*, n.d., <http://www.nida.nih.gov/ResearchReports/Inhalants/Inhalants2.html> (November 27, 2004).

5. "Guidelines for Medical Examiners, Coroners and Pathologists: Determining Inhalant Deaths," *National Inhalant Prevention Coalition*, n.d., <http://www.inhalants.org/final_medical.htm> (January 10, 2005).

6. "What Is Multiple Sclerosis?" *All About Multiple Sclerosis*, May 28, 2003, <http://www.mult-sclerosis.org/whatisms.html> (November 27, 2004).

7. Carl Sherman, "Dopamine Enhancement

Underlies a Toluene Behavioral Effect," *National Institute on Drug Abuse*, vol. 19, no. 5, January 2005, <http://www.nida.nih.gov/MOM/TG/momtg-inhalants.htm> (November 27, 2004).

8. "Guidelines for Medical Examiners, Coroners and Pathologists: Determining Inhalant Deaths," *National Inhalant Prevention Coalition*.

9. "Research Report Series—Inhalant Abuse: What Are Inhalants?" *National Institute on Drug Abuse*.

10. "Huffing: A Continuing Worry," *Child Health Alert, Inc.*, May 1999, p. 2.

11. Carrie Anderson and Glen Loomis, "Recognition and Prevention of Inhalant Abuse," *American Family Physician*, September 1, 2003, vol. 68, issue 5, p. 869.

12. "CADCA Conference Symposium Addresses Re-Emergence of Inhalant Abuse," *Alcoholism and Drug Abuse Weekly*, January 17, 2005, vol. 17, no. 3, p. 1.

13. "Research Report Series—Inhalant Abuse: What Are Inhalants?" *National Institute on Drug Abuse*.

14. "General Background Information: Inhalants" *National Inhalant Prevention Coalition*, n.d., <http://www.inhalants.org/guidelines.htm> (January 10, 2005).

15. *Nation's Health*, May 2004, vol. 34, issue 4, p. 20.

16. "Guidelines for Medical Examiners, Coroners and Pathologists: Determining Inhalant Deaths," *National Inhalant Prevention Coalition*.

Chapter 3. Inhaling History

1. William Broad, "For Delphic Oracle, Fumes and Visions," *New York Times*, March 19, 2002, p. F–1.

2. Ibid.

3. Ibid.

4. Edward M. Brecher, *Licit and Illicit Drugs; The Consumers Union Report on Narcotics, Stimulants, Depressants, Inhalants* (Boston: Little, Brown and Co., 1972), p. 312.

5. Ibid.

6. Ibid.

7. Ibid.

8. Debasish Basu, Om Jhirwal, et al., "Inhalant Abuse by Adolescents: A New Challenge for Indian Physicians," *Indian Journal of Medical Science*, vol. 58, no. 6, June 2004, p. 245.

Chapter 4. Sniffing Death

1. *Alcoholism and Drug Abuse Weekly*, October 11, 2004, p. 6.

2. Cate Baily, "Inhalants," *Scholastic*, n.d., <http:// teacher.scholastic.com/scholasticnews/indepth/

headsup/drug-inhalants.htm> (December 27, 2004).

3. *Family Practice News*, June 1, 2004, vol. 34 issue 11, p. 55.

4. "Non-profit Alliance says class of '79 fails parenting test for drug education," *Science Letter*, April 26, 2005.

5. *Clinical Reference Systems*, Annual 2002, p. 1809.

6. Glenn A. Loomis, *American Family Physician*, September 1, 2003, vol. 68, issue 5, p. 869.

7. "Teens increasingly passing up drugs, cigarettes, survey finds," *Oregonian*, December 22, 2004, p. C-10.

8. "Guidelines for Medical Examiners, Coroners and Pathologists: Determining Inhalant Deaths," *National Inhalant Prevention Coalition*, n.d., <http://www.inhalants.org/final_medical.htm> (January 10, 2005).

9. *Family Practice News*, June 1, 2004.

10. "Teen Drug Use Declines 2003–2004 But Concerns Remain About Inhalants and Pain Killers," *National Institute on Drug Abuse*, December 21, 2004, <http://www.drugabuse.gov/Newsroom/04/NR12-21.html> (January 10, 2005).

11. Joseph T. Sakai, Shannon K. Hall, et al. "Inhalant Use, Abuse and Dependence Among Adolescent Patients" *Journal of the Academy of*

Child and Adolescent Psychiatry, September 2004, vol. 43, issue 9, p. 1080.

12. Aaron M. White, "Brain Development During Adolescence," Duke University, n.d., <http://www.duke.edu/-amwhite/Adolescence/adolescent3.html> (December 27, 2004).

13. Personal interview with Dr. Ken Ensroth, medical director for child and adolescent psychiatry at Legacy Emmanuel Hospital in Portland, Oregon, February 1, 2005.

14. Sakai, Hall, et al., p. 1080.

15. Ibid.

16. "Intelligence Brief: Huffing—The Abuse of Inhalants," *National Drug Intelligence Center*, November 2001, <http://www.usdoj.gov/ndic/pubs07/708/#What> (January 10, 2005).

17. "Guidelines for Medical Examiners, Coroners and Pathologists: Determining Inhalant Deaths," *National Inhalant Prevention Coalition*.

18. *Child Health Alert*, May 1992.

19. Michael Amon, "'Huffing' Blamed in Teen's Death," *Washington Post*, March 22, 2002, p. B5.

20. "Guidelines for Medical Examiners, Coroners and Pathologists: Determining Inhalant Deaths," *National Inhalant Prevention Coalition*.

21. Ibid.

22. Personal interview with John Mitchell, director of Calvert County Substance Abuse Services, January 26, 2005.

23. Craig C. Freudenrich, "How Alcohol Works," *How Stuff Works*, n.d., <http://science.howstuffworks.com/alcohol.htm> (January 10, 2005).

24. "General Background Information: Inhalants," *National Inhalant Prevention Coalition*, n.d., <http://www.inhalants.org/guidelines.htm> (January 10, 2005).

Chapter 5. Huffing Toward Disaster

1. Glenn A. Loomis, *American Family Physician*, September 1, 2003, vol. 68, issue 5, p. 869.

2. Cate Baily, "Pain Meets Poison," *Junior Scholastic*, March 14, 2003, vol. 105, p. 18.

3. Ibid.

4. Personal interview with Dr. Ken Ensroth, medical director for child and adolescent psychiatry at Legacy Emmanuel Hospital in Portland, Oregon, February 1, 2005.

5. "CADCA Conference Symposium Addresses Re-Emergence of Inhalant Abuse," *Alcoholism and Drug Abuse Weekly*, January 17, 2005, vol. 17, no. 3, p. 1.

6. "Huffing: A Continuing Worry," *Child Health Alert*, May 1992, p. 2.

7. Personal interview with Dr. Ken Ensroth, medical director for child and adolescent

psychiatry at Legacy Emmanuel Hospital in Portland, Oregon, February 1, 2005.

8. Lt. Pilowsky Wu and W. E. Schlenger, "Inhalant Abuse and dependence among adolescents in the United States," *Journal of the Academy of Child and Adolescent Psychiatry*, September 2004, vol. 43, issue 9, p. 1206.

9. "General Background Information: Inhalants," *National Inhalant Prevention Coalition*, n.d., <http://www.inhalants.org/guidelines.htm> (January 10, 2005).

10. Ibid.

11. Personal interview with Dr. Ken Ensroth, medical director for child and adolescent psychiatry at Legacy Emmanuel Hospital in Portland, Oregon, February 1, 2005.

12. Ibid.

13. *Alcoholism and Drug Abuse Weekly*, January 5, 2005, p. 1.

14. Ibid.

15. Ibid.

16. Personal interview with Dr. Ken Ensroth, medical director for child and adolescent psychiatry at Legacy Emmanuel Hospital in Portland, Oregon, February 1, 2005.

17. Wu and Schlenger, "Inhalant Abuse and dependence among adolescents in the United States."

18. "Lowes sets policy to limit the sale of potential

inhalants," *Alcoholism and Drug Abuse Weekly*, June 2, 2003, vol. 15, issue 21, p. 8.

19. Ibid.

Chapter 6. New Hope

1. Sean McCollum, "Kids are putting their lives at risk by huffing," *Scholastic Choices*, April 1, 2005, vol. 20, no. 6, p. 18.

2. Ibid.

3. Personal interview with Dr. Ken Ensroth, medical director for child and adolescent psychiatry at Legacy Emmanuel Hospital in Portland, Oregon, February 1, 2005.

4. "Historical Data: The Birth of A.A. and Its Growth in U.S./Canada," n.d., <http://www.alcoholics-anonymous.org> (February 2, 2005).

5. Personal interview with John Mitchell, director of Calvert County Substance Abuse Services, January 26, 2005.

6. Ibid.

7. "General Background Information: Inhalants," *National Inhalant Prevention Coalition*, n.d., <http://www.inhalants.org/guidelines.htm> (January 10, 2005).

8. Pamela Jumper-Thurman and Fred Beauvis, "Treatment of Volatile Solvent Abusers," *NIDA Research Monograph 129 Inhalant Abuse: A Volatile Research Agenda 1992*, p. 203.

9. Personal interview with Dr. Ken Ensroth,

medical director for child and adolescent psychiatry at Legacy Emmanuel Hospital in Portland, Oregon, February 1, 2005.

10. Personal interview with John Mitchell, Director of Calvert County Substance Abuse Services, January 26, 2005.

11. Debasish Basu, Om Jhirwal, et al., "Inhalant Abuse by Adolescents: A New Challenge for Indian Physicians," *Indian Journal of Medical Science*, vol. 58, no. 6, June 2004, p. 248.

12. "General Background Information: Inhalants," *National Inhalant Prevention Coalition*.

13. "Treatment for Inhalant Abuse May Be On the Horizon," *Addiction Professional*, November 2004. vol. 2, issue 6, p. 601.

14. Ibid.

15. "CADCA Conference Symposium Addresses Re-Emergence of Inhalant Abuse," *Alcoholism and Drug Abuse Weekly*, January 17, 2005, vol. 17, no. 3, p. 1.

16. Personal interview with John Mitchell, director of Calvert County Substance Abuse Services, January 26, 2005.

FURTHER READING

Books

Aretha, David. *Inhalants*. Berkeley Heights, N.J.: MyReportLinks.com Books, 2005.

Aronson, Virginia. *How to Say No*. Philadelphia, Penn.: Chelsea House Publishers, 2000.

Graves, Bonnie. *Drug Use and Abuse*. Mankato, Minn.: LifeMatters, 2000.

Hyde, Margaret O., and John F. Setaro. *Drugs 101: An Overview for Teens*. Brookfield, Conn.: Twenty-First Century Books, 2003.

Kozar, Richard. *How to Get Help*. Philadelphia, Penn.: Chelsea House Publishers, 2000.

Internet Addresses

INHALANTS.DRUGABUSE.GOV
Inhalant Abuse:
 <http://inhalants.drugabuse.gov>
 Learn more about inhalants.

National Inhalant Prevention Coalition
 <http://www.inhalants.org>
 Read more about inhalants and the dangers of huffing.

INDEX